MINECRAFT:
Enchanting and Potion Brewing

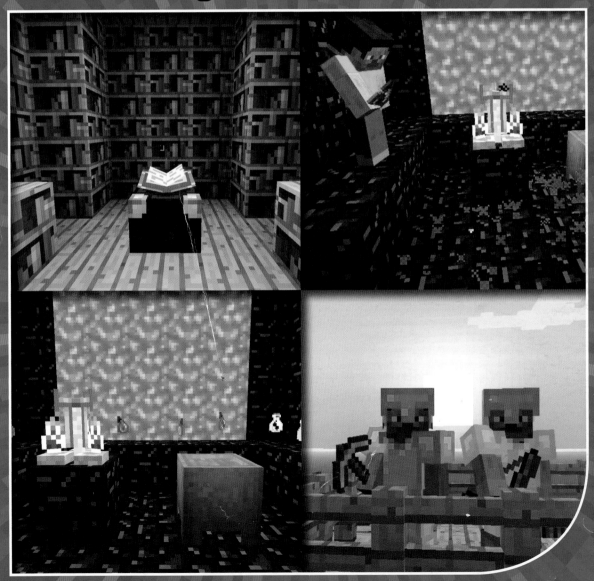

CHERRY LAKE PUBLISHING • ANN ARBOR, MICHIGAN

by James Zeiger

A Note to Adults: Please review the instructions for the activities in this book before allowing children to do them. Be sure to help them with any activities you do not think they can safely complete on their own.

A Note to Kids: Be sure to ask an adult for help with these activities when you need it. Always put your safety first!

Published in the United States of America by Cherry Lake Publishing
Ann Arbor, Michigan
www.cherrylakepublishing.com

Reading Adviser: Marla Conn, Read With Me Now
Photo Credits: Cover and pages 4 and 29, James Zeiger; pages 5 and 22, Piper Keltner; pages 6–8, 17, 20, and 27–28, Sebastian Olsen; page 11, Ares C.; pages 13–14, 16, 19, and 24–25, Jennifer Zeiger.

Library of Congress Cataloging-in-Publication Data
Library of Congress Cataloging-in-Publication data on file.

Cherry Lake Publishing would like to acknowledge the work of The Partnership for 21st Century Skills. Please visit www.p21.org for more information.

Printed in the United States of America
Corporate Graphics

Contents

Chapter 1

A Bit of Magic

A Minecrafter should always be improving. Experience, better materials and tools, and more effective techniques all propel a player through the game. In real life, we can make tools stronger by using harder, longer-lasting materials. The same is true in *Minecraft*. Strong armor protects. Sharp weapons defend. Tough tools get the job done. Leather armor is good, but chainmail armor is better.

Once you've mastered some of the basics, such as building, you can move on to more magical activities.

Enchanted weapons can help you fight dangerous enemies like zombie pigmen!

Diamond swords cause more damage than iron ones. Stone tools last longer than wooden ones.

You also improve as you gain experience and learn the best ways to do each task. You become a better fighter and a better builder. In *Minecraft*, you can even improve beyond what is possible in real life. In this game, magic is very real. Potions and spells bring a touch of **supernatural** help. Have you ever wanted to breathe underwater or shoot flaming arrows from your bow? What if you could progress through *Minecraft* faster? Lava pools wouldn't harm you, and you could be invisible to creatures. Your tools could last forever. Or your sword could be especially deadly to spiders.

One way to use magic is through **enchantment**. Enchanting gives your tools the extra push to take on the next level of challenges. This is where all those experience points you gain fighting and working come into play. You invest them into magical abilities for your tools, weapons, armor, and even books. Simply add a precious mineral called lapis lazuli, open a special enchantment book, and you're set.

Enchantments can give your fishing pole a bit of luck.

What if you could swim for an extended time without coming up for air?

You can also provide your character with tempo-rary superhuman abilities. You can be faster, stronger, invisible, or even immune to fire. And that's not all. There are many types of potions that can help you or harm your enemy. These abilities will come from careful potion brewing. Go on quests to track down rare ingredients. Then combine them in a certain order. Store them away in glass bottles, then take them out and drink them down at just the right time.

In the coming pages, you'll read more about these magical tools. Learn to harness these powers, and you can bring your *Minecraft* character to superhero status.

Chapter 2

Enchanting Basics

As you play *Minecraft*, you'll eventually reach a point where your tools can't be improved any further with new **ores**. This is a perfect time to try your hand at enchanting. Most tools, weapons, and armor can be enchanted in a range of ways. Any of these items can be made more effective. Your character's armor can become better at protecting. This could be a general enchantment against all types of

An enchanted sword could make a big difference!

attacks. Or the armor could become especially effective against specific dangers, such as fire or blasts. You can also give your weapons special abilities, like lighting your arrows on fire. You can add thorns to your character's armor or make your tools last forever. Enchantments can even give you luck! For example, if you add a luck enchantment to your fishing pole, you'll be more likely to catch better fish.

You can obtain enchanted items without making them yourself. Sometimes, villagers will trade them to you in return for emeralds. You may even occasionally snag an enchanted item when you go fishing. You can also pick them up battling zombies, skeletons, or the zombie pigmen of the Nether world. If these creatures are carrying enchanted items when you defeat them, you can pick them up.

Why rely on chance, however, when you can enchant items yourself? There are a couple of ways you can do this. An enchanting table is a good place to start. This table requires a few **exotic** resources to build.

You will need four blocks of obsidian, two diamonds, and a book. In your crafting table, place the book in the top center square. One block of obsidian goes in the center space just below it. Place the other three obsidian blocks in the three spaces of the bottom row. One diamond goes in the center left square, the other in the center right square. After you place the table, you can mine it and collect it **intact**. This allows you to move it if you ever want to.

The table is ready to use immediately. However, its influence on your items might be limited at first. Your experience points determine its abilities. Luckily, these points are a renewable resource. You spend them on enchantments, but you can always make more of them by mining, building, and fighting. The more experience you have, the better your enchantments can be. However, keep in mind that there is no guarantee that an enchantment will be as strong as you want it to be. Enchantments are random. They are limited to your level of experience. Any enchantments at or below that level are fair game, so you cannot predict what level you'll get.

Experience isn't the only thing that improves your chances with the enchantment table. Books can also

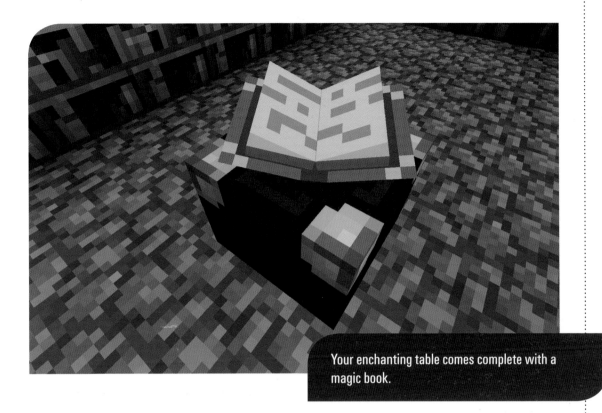

Your enchanting table comes complete with a magic book.

increase a table's abilities. Surround the table with bookshelves and the table will take power from them. Then the table will tend to offer higher-level enchantments. You can craft a bookshelf by combining books and wood blocks. Place your bookshelf within two blocks of the enchanting table. You'll know it's working when you see small **runes** floating from the bookshelves to the table. The more bookshelves you place around your table, the larger the effect will be. You can even stack bookshelf blocks two high. Arrange them in an almost complete circle around the table, too. Just be sure to leave an opening so you can squeeze through.

To enchant an item, click on the table with the Use action. In the enchanting menu, place the item into the empty box on the left, below the book. Add between one and three pieces of lapis lazuli. If your item is able to be enchanted, three enchantment options will pop up in the list on the right. Each option has a number next to it. That number is the experience level you have to spend to perform the enchantment. These can range from one to three levels. Select the enchantment you want. The listed number is subtracted from your total experience points. Then the enchanted item will have the new ability listed. It might also have a few extra ones! Sometimes the table gives extra, unexpected enchantments along with the one listed. The item's name is automatically updated with any new abilities. This way, you can find it in your supplies whenever you need it.

One particularly useful item to enchant is a book. When exploring, you may come across enchanted books in chests. You can also make them yourself with your enchanting table. The books themselves don't do anything directly. What they do is store an

You are given three options for enchantments when you use the enchanting table.

enchantment for later use. This can be a huge benefit. When you enchant a crafted item with the table, you do not know what exactly enchantment perks your item will receive. This is because you don't know which enchanting options will appear ahead of time. So enchanting an item consists partly of luck. However, when you enchant a book, the book will show the specific enchantment it holds in its item description. Sometimes this can give you the information you need to make better decisions about how to enchant a certain item.

Another way to enchant items is to use an anvil. An anvil is a multiuse tool. One use is repairing regular items such as tools, weapons, and armor. Open the anvil's menu by clicking it with the Use button. Then place a broken or worn-down item in one box. Place another of the same item or an ingredient used in making the item into the second box. The anvil combines these items. This allows your tool, weapon, or piece of armor to last longer. You can also rename an item this way. Just place the item you want to rename in the first box. Then edit the name in the box at the top.

Like most of your tools, an anvil wears down over time.

Covering the Cost

Any action you complete using the anvil costs experience points. Once you place items in each of the slots, the menu displays how many experience points the action will cost. You can either accept it or remove the items from their slots. The fancier the tools or higher the enchantments, the more expensive it is to use the anvil. But there is a limit to these costs. If the action costs 40 experience points or more, the anvil won't even give you the option of doing it. The display will just say it is too expensive!

The anvil's other use is in adding or combining enchantments. You can do this in one of two ways. One way is to combine two enchanted items. The other is to combine an item with an enchanted book. Both methods work much like repairing regular objects. By placing one enchanted item in each slot, the anvil combines them into one item with both sets of enchantments. They just have to be the same type of item. For example, you can combine two enchanted pickaxes. But you can't combine an enchanted pickaxe with an enchanted sword.

If you use an enchanted book, the book's enchantment is added to the item. The item can be a regular item or one that is already enchanted. The enchantments held by these books can only be used once. However, you will know exactly what enchantment you'll be adding to an item ahead of time.

Be careful, though. If you're working with an item that is already enchanted, the anvil menu's other box needs to contain something that is also enchanted. This may be an enchanted book or another of the same item that is also enchanted. Otherwise, you'll lose any enchantments you had on your item.

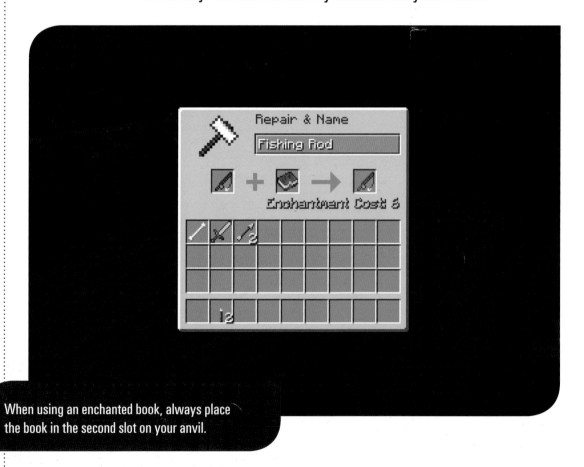

When using an enchanted book, always place the book in the second slot on your anvil.

Chapter 3

Into the Nether

When you first begin a new game in *Minecraft*, you enter a world where you can build, mine, fight, and farm. The sun rises and sets. Sometimes it rains. At other times, the sun shines. But what if you learned there was a world you hadn't seen yet? This alternate world is a lot like the one you know. The hills and valleys are the same. So are the cliffs and islands. But unlike this Overworld, the alternate world is always dark. Strange, tentacled creatures called

Blazes are dangerous enemies that shoot fireballs.

blazes and ghasts live there. The soil is different, and the living things that grow in it are different.

This place is called the Nether. The Nether is dangerous. However, it is absolutely necessary for you to visit if you want to make potions. It is the only place in the game where you can find what you need to brew even the most basic creations.

You'll need a Nether **portal** to reach the Nether. To build one, stack obsidian in a frame that is at least four blocks long and five blocks tall. If you have the materials, you can make it as large as 23 by 23 blocks. You only need the the outer border of blocks. Leave the middle empty. Once the frame is ready, throw fire in to light the portal. The easiest way to do this is probably with flint and steel. You can also use a fire charge or any fire that spreads into the portal. A fireball launched by an attacking ghast or blaze also works. If everything is set up correctly, the center of the frame will light up purple. Step in, wait a few

Quick Tip: Cutting Corners

Do you want to save on materials? Don't include blocks in the corners of your portal's frame. A Nether portal still works even if it's missing its four outer corners.

You'll know your Nether portal is working when the center glows purple.

seconds, and you'll step out into the Nether. The game automatically creates another Nether portal there. You can use this to get back to the portal you built in the Overworld.

Once in the Nether, you can gather the materials you need to start brewing potions. The two most important items to look for are a blaze rod and Nether wart. A blaze rod forms the basis of your brewing stand, on which you'll mix all your potions. Blaze rods are often dropped by blazes when they die, so you'll have to take on at least one of these enemies. Gather more than one blaze rod to be able to make blaze powder. This is one extra ingredient for potions.

Nether wart is a plant that only grows in soul sand, which is found in the Nether. This plant is the first ingredient in nearly every potion. You can find Nether warts at a Nether fortress. Look for them inside the

Nether wart naturally grows in Nether fortresses.

fortress by a central staircase. You can gather them the same way you gather any other crop. If you can, pick up some soul sand, too. Place that soul sand in the ground when you're back in the Overworld. Then you can start farming your own Nether wart there.

You should also keep an eye out for glowstone, magma cubes, and ghasts while you're in the Nether. Glowstone is a material that glows brightly. It most often occurs in high, difficult-to-reach places in the Nether. Sometimes you can also find it near lava. Glowstone is an ingredient in some potions. Magma cubes are dangerous creatures that try to crush their enemies. Kill one, and it may drop magma cream, another material handy for potion brewing. Ghasts are the source of another common potion ingredient: ghast tears. Ghasts sometimes drop these objects when they die. They also occasionally drop gunpowder, which is also used in certain potions. However, you can also obtain gunpowder by killing creepers in the Overworld.

Once you've gathered your supplies, head back to the Nether portal. Step inside, and you'll travel back to the Overworld.

Chapter 4

Brewing Basics

Now that you have the necessary supplies from the Nether, you can get down to brewing business. Through the art of potion brewing, you control the exact effects of your creations. You do this by mixing ingredients in a certain order. Their effects range widely. Some potions can be brewed to make your character stronger. Others assist you in fighting creatures. There are potions to make your character

A brewing stand is an essential part of potion creation.

faster or healthier. Other potions poison, slow, or weaken enemies.

To start, you will need a brewing stand, at least three glass bottles, and a source of water. Remember that blaze rod you fought to get in the Nether? It will form the basis of your brewing stand. Open your crafting table and place the blaze rod in the center square. Add three cobblestones, one in each of the squares along the bottom row. Once it is crafted, place the brewing stand wherever you'll be doing your brewing. Now craft a few glass bottles. Each bottle is made from three glass blocks. One goes in the center left square, one in the center right, and one in the center bottom.

You'll need a water source nearby. For any potion, you'll need to fill three glass bottles with water as your first step. The Use action fills the glass bottles with water. Water bottles can't be stacked, so make sure there is room in your inventory to hold at least three of them.

If there is a lake or similar body of water nearby, you can use that. You can also dig a well. A well needs to be at least two blocks long, two blocks wide, and one block deep. Pour two buckets of water into opposite corners of the hole to fill it. Add a border of building blocks around the outside if you want to make it more attractive. A well provides a never-ending source of water.

Another option for a water source is a cauldron. This can be good if you really want to get into the spirit of potion brewing! It only fills three bottles before you have to refill it. However, it certainly does look witchy. The one time you'll need a cauldron instead of some other water source is if you're brewing potions in the Nether. It's the only water source that works there. To craft a cauldron, place seven iron

You'll need a cauldron if you plan to brew potions while in the Nether. Make sure you bring buckets of water along.

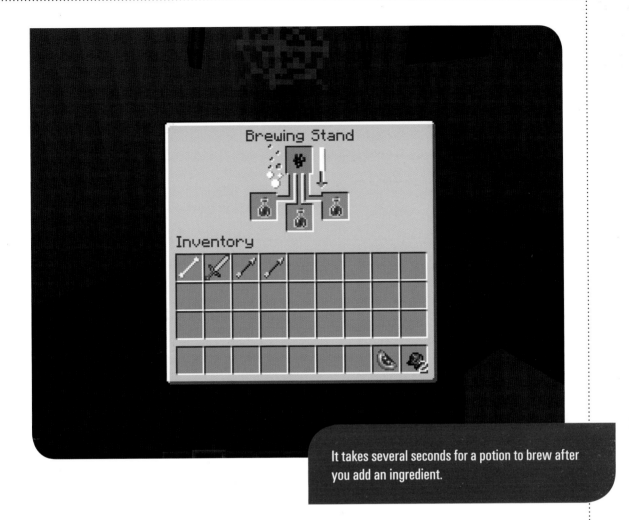

It takes several seconds for a potion to brew after you add an ingredient.

ingots down the left side, across the bottom, and up the right side of your crafting table. You can also go searching for a cauldron in a witch's hut.

Every potion starts with one Nether wart and three bottles of water. This creates the Awkward potion. This potion is your basis for nearly all other potions. To make the Awkward potion, open up the brewing stand's menu with the Use button. At the top of the menu are four boxes. You'll see an outline of a glass

The Right Ingredients

Here are some common basic ingredients you can add to your Awkward potion. Each has its own particular effect:

- Sugar (from sugarcane): speed
- Glistering melon (from gold nuggets and melon slices): healing
- Puffer fish (fished): ability to breathe under water
- Rabbit's foot (dropped by rabbits): jumping
- Golden carrot (from gold nuggets and carrots): night vision
- Ghast tear (dropped by ghasts): "regeneration," or extreme healing
- Blaze powder (from blaze rods): strength
- Magma cream (dropped by magma cubes): fire resistance
- Spider eye (dropped by regular and cave spiders): poison

bottle in each of the bottom three boxes. Place your three water bottles in these. Add the Nether wart to the top box, and the brewing begins. Over the next few seconds, the bubbles to the left of your ingredients will light up. The arrow to the right will slowly fill. When the process is complete, what once were three bottles of water will be three bottles of Awkward potion.

Awkward potion doesn't do anything on its own. The ingredients you add to it give the potion its effect. The effects of most basic potions last three minutes.

A few special ingredients can be added to your potions for bonus abilities. Glowstone dust makes a potion's effects stronger. Add redstone dust to make the effects last longer. Fermented spider eye corrupts most potions. Generally, this means the potion's effects are reversed. A potion for strength becomes a potion for weakness. Healing potions become harmful. A potion made for speed turns into one that slows the player down.

Most potions are made for you to drink.

There are a couple of exceptions. The effect of poison is increased, for example, rather than reversed. Night vision potion turns into an invisibility potion. You can also turn a potion into a weapon by adding gunpowder. Gunpowder makes certain potions into splash potions. These creations can be thrown at enemies. The potion lands, splashes, and affects whatever it hits.

There are a lot of different potions you can make by mixing various ingredients in different orders.

You can throw splash potions at enemies to harm or weaken them.

With enchantments and potions ready for use, you can take your game to a whole new level!

Experiment and see what you can create! But be careful—check the label before you try a potion. This will tell you its effects.

Now that you know how to enchant items and brew potions, you can take your *Minecraft* adventures to a whole new level. Where will you go next? What will you build?

Glossary

enchantment (en-CHANT-muhnt) a magical property given to an item

exotic (ig-ZAH-tik) unusual and fascinating, or from a faraway place

ingots (ING-guhts) masses of metal that have been shaped into bars

intact (in-TAKT) whole

ore (OR) rock or soil that contains metal or valuable minerals

portal (POR-tuhl) a large or important entrance

runes (ROONZ) letters from an ancient writing system

supernatural (soo-pur-NATCH-ur-uhl) having to do with magic

Find Out More

BOOKS

Miller, Megan. *The Ultimate Unofficial Encyclopedia for Minecrafters: An A–Z of Tips and Tricks the Official Guides Don't Teach You.* New York: Skyhorse Publishing, Inc., 2015.

O'Brien, Stephen. *The Ultimate Player's Guide to Minecraft.* Indianapolis: Que Publishing, 2015.

WEB SITES

DigMinecraft—Brewing Recipes in Minecraft

www.digminecraft.com/brewing_recipes/index.php
Step-by-step recipes for a range of potions make this site very handy.

Minecraft101—Brewing Potions

www.minecraft101.net/r/brewing-potions.html
Read a basic how-to on brewing potions. The site also has links to recipes and tips for obtaining ingredients.

Minecraft Enchantment Calculator

www.minecraftenchantmentcalculator.com/rev6/
Do you want an idea of what an enchantment will cost ahead of time? Use this calculator!

Minecraftopia—Minecraft Enchantments

www.minecraftopia.com/minecraft_enchantments
Visit this site for a brief description on what enchantments are and how to do them. There's also a list of types of enchantments you can do.

Index

About the Author

James Zeiger is a student at the Missouri University of Science and Technology. An avid gamer, his lifelong interest in engineering naturally led him to Minecraft.